Connor Allen

Connor is the newly appointed Children's Laureate of Wales (2021-2023). Since graduating from Trinity Saint David as an Actor, he has worked with companies such as Sherman Theatre, Tin Shed Theatre and National Theatre Wales.

He is a member of National Youth Theatre of Great Britain and was also the winner of TriForce's Cardiff MonologueSlam, representing Wales at the London winners edition. As a writer he was a member of the BBC Wales Welsh Voices and The Welsh Royal Court writing groups and has written for BBC Wales, BBC Radio 4, Sherman Theatre, Literature Wales and Dirty Protest.

Connor's work is heavily inspired by elements of his own life such as grief, love, masculinity, identity, and ethnicity.

Most recently he was longlisted for the 2020 Wales Writer in Residence, won the 2021 Rising Star Wales Award and was a Jerwood Live Work Fund recipient in 2021. He is associate artist of his hometown theatre The Riverfront in Newport.

First published in the UK in 2022 by Aurora Metro Publications Ltd
80 Hill Rise, Richmond, TW10 6UB
www.aurorametro.com   info@aurorametro.com
twitter @aurorametro FB/AuroraMetroBooks

Production: Yasmeen Doogue-Khan

Printed in the UK by 4edge Ltd. on sustainably resourced paper.
ISBN: 978-1-912430-85-7
ISBN: 978-1-912430-86-4

THE MAKING OF A MONSTER

BY
CONNOR ALLEN

AURORA METRO BOOKS

WALES MILLENNIUM CENTRE

Wales Millennium Centre is a home for the arts in Wales, a cauldron of creativity for the nation. They fire imaginations by creating their own theatre productions, festivals and digital experiences – as well as curating world-class, critically acclaimed touring productions – from musical theatre and comedy to dance and cabaret. They kindle emerging talents with their own fresh, provocative and popular productions, rooted in Welsh culture. They're also a charity, collaborating with organisations, communities and young people to make the arts accessible to everyone. They ignite a passion for the arts with life-changing learning experiences and chances to shine in the spotlight.

Thanks to all the staff at Wales Millennium Centre.

THE MAKING OF A MONSTER

CREATIVE TEAM

Connor Allen	Writer, Concept, Performer
Conrad Murray	Director
Oraine Johnson	Composer, Music Producer, Performer
David Bonnick Jr	Performer and Additional Material
Krystal S. Lowe	Movement Director
TK Hay	Set Designer
Leo Flint	Video Designer
Luke Davies	Video Designer Assistant/ Animator
Zeynep Kepekli	Lighting Designer
Kiera Liberati	Stylist

PRODUCTION TEAM

Harry Abbott	Stage Manager
Daniel Taylor	Production Manager
Eren Celikdemir	Lighting Programmer
Sacha van Zutphen	Dresser/Wardrobe Assistant
Sian Owens	Captions Operator
Gwilym Huws	Video Programmer
Marcus Wareham	Projectionist
Daniel Trenchard	Video Engineer
Cara Walker	Emerging Artist Placement
Orique Johnson	Sound Op
Sam Lewis	Prody LX
Vada Baldwin	Scenic Artist
Wabriya King	Dramatherapist

BIOGRAPHIES

Conrad Murray – Director

Conrad Murray is a theatre maker, director, musician, writer and composer. As artistic director, he has led the BAC Beatbox Academy for the last decade, innovating in hip hop/ beatbox theatre with various projects.

His last major production 'Frankenstein: How to Make a Monster' got 5 star reviews from *The Stage*, *The Guardian* and others. It won the Off West End award, Total Theatre award, and won pick of the fringe at the Adelaide Fringe Festival. It was adapted into a BBC film in 2020.

'Pilots' Crongton Knights' (Musical Director) was picked as one of the top theatre shows of the year by *The Guardian* in 2020.

He was chosen as part of *The Stage*'s top 100 people in their 2020 list which highlighted his show 'High Rise eState of Mind' with his theatre company Beats & Elements, and a finalist in The Arts Foundation's theatre makers category.

Current projects include - new 'BAC Beatbox Academy hip -hop theatre show for kids' based on 'The Pied Piper' for Batt-ersea Arts Centre 2023. He was recently Beatbox Coach on Giles Terera's 'The Meaning Of Zong' for the Bristol Old Vic.

He is musical director, lyricist and composer for Roy Williams' adaptation of Michael Rosen's 'Unexpected Twist' (2023).

In 2022, his first published works were published by Bloomsbury/Methuen Drama, 'Making Hip Hop Theatre - Beatbox & Elements'.

He has collaborated and/or made work for various venues and institutions including Battersea Arts Centre, The National Theatre Studio, The Lyric Hammersmith, Mountview School of Theatre Arts, The Tate, Royal Central School of Speech and Drama, Camden People's Theatre, Roundhouse, Theatre Royal Stratford East, UCL, The Courtyard Theatre.

Oraine Johnson – Composer, Music Producer & Performer

Oraine Johnson is an actor, writer, composer, and singer. He trained at the Birmingham Theatre School (BA Hons in Acting).

Oraine's credits for TV include BBC 'Danny and the Human Zoo' (BBC) and 'Choices' (Channel 4), as well as award-winning short films 'Repercussions' and 'Domino Effect'. He has toured nationally and internationally with theatre shows, including critically-acclaimed 'The Tin Violin', 'Richard III', 'Jungle Book' and an award-winning production of 'One Flew Over the Cuckoo's Nest'. He is a multi-instrumental musician and has composed for the National Theatre and produced for major grime recording artists. His songs have been rotated on BBC 1xtra, WM and other national and commercial radio stations.

From MTV to performing at the NEC and O2 arena in London, Oraine has navigated his way through an industry which still struggles with representation and diversity. Therefore it was only natural for him to create and write content to be the change that he wants to see: to create stories that represented him and his upbringing.

'Lucid: The Dreamwalker' was created by Oraine to deliver a unique and fresh story that would be able to expand as a franchise into the world of comics, novels, games and music. Oraine has recently signed a multi-book and audio deal with a major publishing house set for worldwide release in early 2024.

David Bonnick Jnr – Performer & Additional Material

David is an actor from South London. He trained at Mountview Drama School graduating with a BA in Acting.

David has appeared in 'EastEnders' and played Bobby Brown in the Whitney Houston & Bobby Brown 'Addicted to Love' documentary on TV. He has featured in a number of commercials including the Tesco Christmas advert and for Carphone Warehouse. Theatre includes 'The Day the Waters Came', 'Scratched Out', 'High Rise eState of Mind', and 'All My Sons' at the Queens Theatre in Hornchurch. He was a member of the Young People's Theatre at the BAC and worked on a number of scratch shows and main house productions.

David is also a rap artist and has recorded music which is streamed on all music services. He also performs at gigs and music festivals such as Boomtown, Wilderness, I Luv Live and other hip-hop events.

All Jonny's battle rap lines in *Monster* are written by David.

Connor Allen

Conrad Murray

David Bonnick Jr. & Connor Allen

Oraine Johnson

AUTHOR'S NOTE

To Mum,
Thank you
For never giving up on me

What do I even say or how do I start an author's note is what's going through my mind as I write this.

Think Con, Think of something witty and really good to write. But I can't think of anything. Mind's blank.

I mean the fact I'm even in a position to be writing an author's note for a published script is insane and I hope that it offers hope to other people out there that your story matters and needs to be told.

Growing up I thought I was alone in a lot of my questions and thoughts. But the older I've got and the more I speak to others, I realise that I wasn't the only one who felt *not enough.* So what I'm saying is that I hope *Monster* can be a way of understanding that we all have questions and insecurities, we all feel how we feel and that's ok.

We are human and we make mistakes.

Monster came out of the exploration and subsequent understanding of my teenage years and I have to thank Julia, Kully and Emma from the bottom of my heart for believing in a mixed-race kid from a council estate and encouraging him to believe that his story and experience matters.

And from their nurture, knowledge and support, I now pass that on to you, whoever you are reading this. Your stories and your experiences matter.

They make you who you are.

And to Branwen and Justin for coming on this journey with me and having my back and sticking with me through the ups and downs.

I've so many people to thank (you know who you are) and I always say that *Monster* is the recipe and everyone involved in whatever capacity big or small are the ingredients.

But these people below I have to shout out because I wouldn't have *Monster* and 5 years of development if it wasn't for them.

Julia Thomas

Oraine Johnson

Branwen Davies

Emma Evans

Justin Cliffe

Big Booty Bridget

Nathan Crossan Smith

Bryony Kimmings

Emma Harding

Sam Dabb

Leah Roberts

Olivia Harris

Team Riverfront

Doorstep Arts

Kully Thurai

Lorne Cambell

Debris Stevenson

Tom Bevan

Blade

Rachel Dudley and The Royal Court

My school teachers

Lastly, to Bridget,

Thank you for seeing a monster and loving him anyway.

THE MAKING OF A MONSTER

by

Connor Allen

CHARACTERS

CONNOR
CONNOR, aged 6
CONNOR, aged 15
THE VOID
THE MUSICIAN (ORAINE)
RANDOM GUY
POLICE OFFICER
SOLICITOR
MUM
FATHER
JONNY
ANSWERING MACHINE/NAN
MULTIPLE TEACHERS
A DUCK(S)

The doors are the gateways to the story

The stage is black. A void. Nothing can be seen.

Sounds of tranquil water and glitches fill the void as the audience enters.

They are about to leave reality and take a trip inside Connor's mind. What will they find?

Fragments of his past and present are scattered throughout the void, pieces of him like litter to be picked up. Action Men, afro comb, lottery ticket, condom, teddy bear, thesaurus, birthday balloon, mobile phones etc.

A sealed padlocked steel door briefly appears at the back. It's vibrating with a deep bass and shaking. It's making a noise and trying to open from the other side.

The sealed door disappears.

Stairs

CONNOR (V.O.) Do me a favour all of you
　　　　　　Close your eyes
　　　　　　And Imagine.
CONNOR　　Picture stairs, 13 steps
　　　　　　Red carpet climbing to the top
　　　　　　One large base step at the bottom
　　　　　　you're 6 six years old
　　　　　　Sat at the bottom
　　　　　　A pair of wellies on your feet
　　　　　　A little backpack by your side.
　　　　　　A goody bag and a balloon.
　　　　　　Ready to go
　　　　　　Waiting to go

A promise
Flowing through your body like blood
swimming through your arteries
A promise
keeping you more alive than the blood
or oxygen

Connor explodes onto the stage.

The promise of a day out
The promise of a park
The promise of ducks
The promise of a dad

And time's slowly ticking away
Sat here hoping, wishing he'd stay

Second by second passes by
You think, he'll be here in a minute, no lie
Tick Tock Tick Tock Tick Tock
Tick Tock Tick Tock Tick Tock

Tick Tock go the hands of the clock
Sat there waiting for the door knock knock
Praying to the powers that be
Dad will arrive like he's won Grand Prix

What's that... we're going to see
The ducks in the lake by the giant oak tree
Feeding them with the bread from the Braces
Looking up at dad with a smile on our faces

I felt so alone
as a toddler hoping dad's on time
at the same time
in my Wellington boots and my rucksack
I'm praying for dad to arrive
Standing waiting
how many times have I heard
that he's on the way

how many times have I heard
don't cry babes
how many times have I
stood by the door
wiping tears away

Been so many years of waiting
but I'm still hopeful
I've cried so many tears
with questions
and got no answers

Dad where are you
Dad how could you
leave me patiently waiting
waiting for you

But seconds become minutes
Minutes become hours
And before you know it, the day's over

And another promise is broken

See you were promised a day out at the park to feed the ducks

But that shouldn't matter because he don't give two fucks

No matter how much mum says he's not coming

You remain hopeful

A promise was made after all

So you stay

On that bottom step all day

No food as you think you'll get food at the park

No playing with your friends outside because you think you'll be playing outside

With your dad

at the park.

Connor is stood in front of the audience. He is here. He is ready.

A wall of TVs is revealed with different scenes from Connor's past, and different elements that make Connor who he is, all playing out on different screens.

Hi there

My name's Connor

And you were all just me

Six years old

That was one of my earliest memories

Of my father

Dad

Breaking yet another promise

Connor walks over to the birthday balloon and stamps on it. A grey duck is revealed inside.

Brief moment. Connor ignores it.

> On my birthday
> my sixth birthday
> Waiting
> You see growing up my father
> *Dad*
> sperm donor
> *Dad*
> whatever
> you want to call him
> He wasn't around
> And that was bare confusing
> It was bare hard

The duck darts across the space. Connor ignores it.

It was...

> So as I said my name's Connor
> I'm 30
> I'm from Newport
> I'm mixed-race
> I'm a man
>
> But I didn't have anyone to teach me that
> Growing up
> To show me what that meant
> being a man
> being mixed-race

It was all really conf/

Glitch. Pause.

Nah wait there. I've already used confusing

Connor looks around inside the void and the scattered litter and picks up the thesaurus and looks through.

Two seconds

Confusing...

Confusing...

The sealed padlocked door appears again at the back. It's vibrating with a deeper bass and shaking. Making a noise and trying to break free as if someone is banging it and trying to open it from the other side.

Connor ignores it. The door disappears.

Ah there's quite a few actually.

So...

being a man

being mixed-race

It was all really *complex*

It was all really *upsetting*

It was all really *complicated*

It was all really *difficult*

You get the picture.

Little bit of history...

1805

Peter Mark Roget

creates an English language thesaurus which has gone on to become known as the 'Roget Thesaurus' published in 1852.

It's updated every year and is still used all over the world to this day.

Let's play a game. I love games. Let's think of different synonyms for certain words and I'll see if they make it to 'Roget's Thesaurus'.

So let's play

I want to draw your attention to the word white or whiteness for a sec.

Who thinks they know some of the synonyms for whiteness?

'Roget's Thesaurus' has over 134 synonyms for whiteness, most with positive connotations such as ... clear, pure, ivory

Now let's look at another. Black or blackness.

Who thinks they know some synonyms for black or blackness?

'Roget's Thesaurus' has over 120 synonyms for black and blackness with barely any positive connotations such as ... dirty, prohibited, bleak.

One side of you is positive and accepted
The other side of you is the opposite

Which am I?

And you're probably thinking

Oh why is Connor going on about words so much?

Words Words Words

I promise you

It will all make sense

Just stick with me

But before all that, before I was on that bottom step in my wellies, before all these synonyms and words, we were at my 6th birthday party yeah? And what's a party without pass the parcel?

2 wrapped parcels are revealed.

So hit that music and let's play pass the parcel.

Music Plays. Music Stops.

Audience member unwraps the parcel. It's an Action Man.

Oh look at that. A bit of nostalgia.

An Action Man.

Let's go again.

Hit it.

Music Plays. Music Stops.

Audience member unwraps the parcel. It's a black Action Man.

Oh look at that

Another Action Man

Loved Action Men growing up.

Connor takes the Action Men and places them in the void.

Can I ask you...

Which Action Man is good?

Which one is ugly?

Which one is beautiful?

Which one is bad?

Which one looks like you?

Another trip down the history books.

1940's America had psychologists Mamie and Kenneth Clark conduct what has become known as the doll test.

They took a group of Black children aged between 3 - 7

Gave them dolls. Both identical except one had white skin with yellow hair and the other had brown skin and black hair.

They asked questions about the dolls like which doll is good? Which doll is bad? Which doll is pretty? Which doll is ugly?

What they found was the majority preferred the white doll and assigned positive connotations towards it. Most disregarded the brown doll and assigned negative traits towards it.

The saddest part of all this is when the children are asked which doll looks like you and after associating the brown doll with ugliness and bad there is hesitation and a realisation as they lean for the brown doll. Those negative traits they attached with the brown doll are attached to their own identity.

Children become race conscious at a very early age

So... Couple that with 'Roget's Thesaurus' and you quickly understand how blackness is a synonym for bad and whiteness is synonymous with beauty and power.

But what does it do for your identity when you have links to both?

A door appears titled 26th June 2007.

It's probably better if I just show you

Take you back

To 2007

He walks through. He's transported back to High School in 2007.

Back to school

26th June 2007, Lliswerry High School.

Music fills the void.

CONNOR   26th June 2007 started off as most school days do.

Left my house about half-seven, gets to school about eight

Stroll through the ugly green gates of the school and round the back to the side of the canteen.

Rinses the boys of a few quid in pitch and toss

before the morning bell rings and registration is a near.

I swagger through the automatic doors of the kingdom and down the hall to the form room.

Strut through the classroom door to see

Different animals in different clutters

Different personalities hanging in flutters

Y'know school can be a real tough place.

Each and every day you gotta keep face.

Cos in there it's like the rules of the jungle

Hyenas lurking around corridors, being proper fungal.

Lions, well, they just reign supreme.

Free

To do what they like.

With the koalas pretty chilled.

With not a care in the world.

Different people from all walks of life grace the school halls

Graffiti and food stains are sprayed over the walls.

But amongst all that you still get one dickhead who thinks he's better than the rest

Thinks he's cooler than school

But thrives in the dog-eat-dog world of the jungle.

The urban jungle that's called school.

And that dickhead is called Jonny.

The resident dickhead of the class.

Nah,

actually the chief wasteman of the whole year.

Always trying to make himself look big.

Targeting someone or another.

Like a predator.

Scouring the jungle

Today's target just so happened to be me.

I felt him loading up for the kill.

In the background just thinking of what to say.

He slithers over

Pops his head over my shoulder

And starts with

JONNY   Yo Con

Did you get a perm when you were younger?

The scene is set and a clash awaits. Bar for bar.

The classroom are on their seats waiting for this.

A montage of grime classics fill the void one after another.
Jonny sets the bar with the first diss.

JONNY   My man went to the barber's
And at the barber's had a hair cut
But the barber that you sat down for blud
He didn't show you love
Your haircut fucked
And your hairline all gone
What the fuck were you thinking Con
Ah Na listen
Your haircut is very convincing

It's only now that I see your vision
And precision
To look like
sideshow bob from the Simpsons
You're a straight beg
Like your mum
She offered man head I was like yep
I can't really say that I didn't enjoy it
There was a bit of annoyances
Like how she gonna talk
With my dick in her mouth
And had her legs open
For me to fuck now

CONNOR   Jonny Jonny Jonny Jonny
you don't want this smoke
You can't cope
I'll have you on the ropes

Abuse you worse than a catholic pope
It's easy cos you're a dope
In prison you'll be dropping the soap
Go to Gretna Green with your mum
Cos me and her are gunna elope
Crikey crikey
Con about to get icy
Listen Jonny don't like me
But he ain't gunna fight

Coming at me
I'll throw your body in the boot of my car
Wait... What... too far? Nah
When I'm through with you
You can go and get devious crew
I'll cook you all brown chicken stew
What are you gunna do?
Nothing
You fake
You fool
Go and draw your tool
Just remember you'll be lying in a pool
Of blood
For talking crud

JONNY Oi
ain't that your mum over there
Oi
ain't that your girl over there
Oi

who's that prick over there?
the brudda name Con right

I heard you got a mixtape coming
When I heard it, rubbish
bare lies that you're from the hood bro,
why are you shook
Wait, hold up a second
Let me ask a question
bro are you really from the ends always on
a hype
chatting shit on the mic
and I'm gonna murk you tonight like
Lloyd Pike
well rest in peace
boy that must of cut deep
now you got no soldiers on your team
you ain't gonna last long
like the life of the queen
homeless begging please
can't even afford to buy Vaseline
for your top lip that's filled with herpes
your girlfriend text me to give her brain
but I'm not a bocat
that's your ting

CONNOR   Jonny you're getting knocked the fuck out
So I recommend you shut the fuck up
It's a cardinal sin out here chatting clout
So I recommend you shut the fuck up
I'll box you to the right side of your jaw

box you down before you hit the floor
I'll stamp you out DEAD stiff on the floor
You wish you just shut the fuck up

Jonny you ain't no killer on the mic
And I'll dead you like my friend Lloyd Pike
Dead in the ground you're making no sound
Killing you is cheap it won't cost me a pound
You're gay cos you got big blow job lips
Out there sucking bare dick for some tips
just like your mum
Huh huh what a whore
Got bare men queuing at her front door

Her door
Her door
Your mother is a whore
Got bare men at her door
Your mum's a fucking whore
What!

JONNY   Who said I can't rhyme
who said I can't spit
man's got hella bars that's sick
man's got hella bars for you prick
and I got skeng loaded with a full clip
like BOOM
shot gun business
I don't care what you heard
or what you witnessed

I don't care what you're gonna do next
cause you're just a lickle boy
with your big man threats like
What me
am I really scared
of the light skin yute
with a perm on his head
while you're at the bus stop
waiting for a bus
I'm on a R1 bike
with your girl on the back
like Mmmm!! (Motorbike sound she felt it)
cause I gave her a ride without the helmet
cause I gave her a ride without L plates
and I buss on her face
no condom

CONNOR   My name's Con I'm the don
Jon should already know where I'm from
Newport and Jamaica this faker's done
This one's for the real ones

Jonny can't harm me
He'll get folded like origami
Middle finger in your girl's punani
She knows my name is Welsh, Jamaican
even Punjabi

Ask your girl bout the last time somebody
made her moan
That was Con

Ask your girl who made her cum all over
the phone

That was Con

Ask your girl who rocked her world who
popped her cherry yo

that was Con

Ask your girl who made her squeal like
Mariah Carey

That was Con

She's screaming my name

Louder louder going insane

A puddle's on my bed

Your girl's pussy's turning red

She's begging me for more

You never made her cum before

Jonny oh my lord

What's that?

You're a fucking FRAUDDDDDD.

The classroom erupts in joy as Connor merks Jonny and wins the clash. Jonny is raging. Standing there vexed.

JONNY   You just keep creating your wannabe dad
in your afro Jackson 5 nappy head of
yours yeah

cos your real one ain't around.

Even that nigga don't want you.

A duck darts across the classroom. Quacks.

CONNOR   And for me that's it.

Football that's the red card
Chess, that's checkmate.
That's Skepta V Devilman

And all I see is red
RAGE.
Uncontrollable rage.
Flowing through my veins.

Before I know it
We're in a scuffle
Dived over the table I got Jonny by the throat
Fists clenched above his head
aiming to pound his jaw.
Sounds of the animals filling the jungle.

Encouragement.
Hesitation.
Anticipation.
Delight.
They all wanna see this fight.

Then Mr Smith our form tutor walks in,
flips his lid.
Can't believe what he's seeing.
Demands to know what's going on.

Silence.

Picks us both up off the floor
Chucks us out the door

Glitch.

Picks us both up off the floor
Chucks us out the door
Silence.
On our way we go.
To the headmaster's office to explain what went down
Jonny's staring at me the entire way.
He's still got that stupid fucking frown.
As we make our way down the corridor up the stairs
I know that it's inevitable.
Jonny and me
Unfinished business see
He's got a reputation to uphold.
So whether it's break, lunch, after school or next week.
Eventually have to do more than just speak
As the door to the headmaster's office draws nearer

Can't help but think how I'm gunna explain this to mum.
She's almost at breaking point
Shit.
She's almost done.

Hair

The void. Connor storms into the barber's with the rage of the memory before.

CONNOR   Yo how long for a haircut!?

Connor sits on the sofa about to get his hair cut, waiting for the barber to set up.

A random guy who is waiting spots Connor and proceeds to make conversation. They both wait.

RANDOM GUY   /Yo bruv

CONNOR   Wassup

RANDOM GUY   You from around here then

CONNOR   Yeah. Just down the road. Corpa boy

RANDOM GUY   Fairs. You look familiar that's all.

CONNOR   Yeah...

RANDOM GUY   Yeah. Like I've seen your face.

CONNOR   Newport a small place

RANDOM GUY   Yeah. You look like someone I know
                [~~father's name[1]~~]

Glitch.

CONNOR   Yeah. He would be my father.

RANDOM GUY   Oh shit. Yeah that makes sense now. You the double of him.

                Double of your old man.

CONNOR   Well don't go screaming that around

RANDOM GUY   You see him lately?

CONNOR   Ain't seen him in years

Barber chair is free. Connor sees an escape.

---

1   Connor's father's name redacted, leaving a blank space for the actor/sound system to fill.

CONNOR   Safe yeah.

RANDOM GUY   Safe.

Have to start calling you Junior as you the double of him

CONNOR   Or don't

Connor gets up and goes to the barber's chair. The barber gown goes around him.

CONNOR   I want a shape up with a little bit off the top

Actually just take it all off. Get this perm off my head.

Time is frozen.

Connor picks up his afro comb and enters a TED Talk style presentation about hair. The information he wished he knew when he was that teenager in the chair.

CONNOR   Hair

A big factor in anyone's identity

But what does it actually mean?

Hair.

On the wider scale

As Connor starts speaking, images of different Black hairstyles and identities are shown on the screens in the background. Slowly filling the void like the hairstyles that have filled Connor's mind over the years. All there on display in their beauty.

It is easy for people to dismiss conversations about hair as something foolish without really or truly understanding the deep, deep significance of hair for many, many people.

The universality of racism and micro-aggressions centred around *Black* hair can indeed be confusing and does indicate that we are, as a country, as the old Great Britain, maybe not as progressive as we like to think.

Stick with me though.

See, in early African civilisations, just about everything about a person's identity could be learnt by looking at their hair

Hairstyles could indicate a person's family background, tribe and social status.

Now *Black* hair has been an integral feature of *Black* history for decades with the likes of Dreadlocks and The Afro to name a few.

Now, The Afro, being a symbol in the 60s of rebellion, pride and empowerment

Most famously rocked by Angela Davis.

Black people took to protest against oppression and segregation during this period

The Afro became an assertion of *Black* identity in contrast to previous trends and fashions that were primarily not *Black*. i.e. White.

It was a symbol of who they were as human beings.

It was a symbol of self empowerment.

It was a symbol of *Black* identity.

The void is full of different Black hairstyles from different people. All different shapes and sizes.

So, *Black* hair and *Black* identity are intrinsically linked.

We can agree on that much now yeah?

And *if Black* hair and *Black* identity are intrinsically linked,

what happens in cases

where the *Black* identifier isn't there?

Is an identity even there?

But I just showed you the start of a story
26th June 2007

I should probably take you back so you can see how this all played out.

Connor goes to travel back through a door to 26th June but the door starts glitching, and the padlocked door reappears but this time it has edged closer.

CONNOR   That's not right

The 26th June I said

A muffled voice can be heard from behind the padlocked door.

No No No

To escape the padlocked door Connor goes in an elevator and frantically presses buttons to run away and go to a different floor.

The elevator starts to move. Elevator music plays as he moves to a different floor.

Come on... *Come on*

Parents' Evening

Stuck in the elevator travelling down. Music still playing. The elevator stops.

15th June 2007. Parents' Evening.

The void and musician become the teachers.

ENGLISH TEACHER Is it just you tonight, Mum?

Right,

Um,

If I could show you two of Connor's test results.

One from before Christmas and the other from last week. The one before Christmas he scored an A grade.

Which is brilliant and well within his capability. The test last week resulted in a C grade.

Both mock tests covering the same material.

So in essence he should be getting consistent grades.

It is no secret that Connor's behaviour has drastically changed over the past months/

CONNOR   /Next

HISTORY TEACHER Simply put Miss Allen, if Connor carries on down the path he is on then those great predicted grades he acquired last year go out of the window.

And I predict he'll be in jail or worse

Pause.

CONNOR   Next

MATHS TEACHER   Miss Allen your son is quite advanced but how do I put it...

He keeps acting up in class

CONNOR   Next

SCIENCE TEACHER Ah, Connor.

Connor, Connor, Connor

Where to start with Connor

CONNOR   Ugh ... Next

GEOGRAPHY TEACHER   Ever the class clown is Connor, Miss Allen

CONNOR   Next!

DRAMA TEACHER Now I can only speak for my class

But Connor has a clear engagement and enjoyment in my class.

It's a pleasure to watch him grow and develop

My only concern would be that I wish he was in more of the classes.

CONNOR   Next!!

WELSH TEACHER Hi Mum.

Is Dad not with you tonight?

CONNOR   *NEXT!*

FORM TEACHER Evening Mum,

Please have a tissue

Now being that I don't teach Connor I'm only his form teacher I can only talk and speak on what he's like in form.

Obviously I hear from other teachers what he's like in their lessons but I only judge by what I'm given.

Connor is nothing but a joy.

And I do mean that Mum.

He's got all the potential and the personality to go with it

But from what I hear, he's too busy trying to be the funniest in the class instead of the hardest worker in the class.

Now I have a lot of time for him as you know Mum but you have to meet us halfway Connor.

There's a reason your mother is here in tears and I've waited until the end to see you both.

It's because we both care and want to help you.

Connor storms out of parents' evening.

Connor wait

CONNOR   Get a grip

I don't need your help. Either of you.

So just leave it yeah

Connor exits. Mum is left crying.

Form teacher calls out to Connor.

FORM TEACHER   Connor

Connorrrrrr

Connor runs from the elevator and back into the void.

He's escaped the padlocked door and is searching for 26th June 2007. Smoke starts to engulf the void.

A door titled 26th June 2007 appears. Sound of Mum calling draws him nearer.

Connor opens the door and enters the memory. Voice of Mum yelling "Connor" fills the space.

The Fight

26th June 2007.

Connor goes through the front door of his house. Stands in the hallway by the shoe rack.

Smell of red velvet cake still fills the house. Voice of Mum yelling "Connor" still filling the space.

CONNOR   Ugh

As the screeching of Mum yelling from the kitchen stabs my ears like a knife

She's still acting like a wannabe housewife Still trying to make

Well, still trying to bake

The perfect red velvet cake and I'm just like for fuck sake

I finish taking off my other Nike and scream back

What?!

Yelling stops.

Mum replies from the kitchen

Don't use that tone with me

What are you doing home so early?

Usually back in time for tea

You shouldn't be home for another half an hour see.

I shout out *Why's it even matter?*

Did I interrupt you and your fancy man
or something?

What, is he in there?

Cos there's a funny smell in here actually
What you guys been doing exactly?

She bursts
Out of the kitchen taking me by surprise
In a foul mood
Like why've I gotta be so rude.

Don't be sarky Connor for goodness' sake
I been in here most of the day making red
velvet cake
I kiss my teeth
roll my eyes
and say yeah well I had revision period last
two lessons
so I was allowed to go home early

Well I hate to burst your bubble
She says to me in a cocky way that can only
mean trouble
But the school have already rung and told
me what went on
And all I'm going to say to you is *you* are
most definitely grounded Con.
And before I can interrupt And tell her
what's up

She's already babbling on about
How enough is enough
It's all getting too much
Too tough
She can't do this anymore
With me constantly being at war
With her
With everyone
Teachers
Brother
The law
And more

I say
Are you gunna let me speak now?
Or are you just gunna carry on?

Cos Mum, I've had your shit, going on at me constantly for weeks
Sounding like all them teachers at parents' evening, a bunch of complete neeks
You're all taking the piss
And I don't need this
I'm not having an existential crisis
Or falling down some abyss
So please yeah, just give it a miss
Because your silence right now would be fucking bliss

She says I'm acting bizarre
Cos I'm out there smashing up cars
She asks me if I'm stable?
As she proceeds to folding clothes around
the kitchen table
Says she's being serious

I say Mum
you're acting fucking delirious

She's not going to watch me throw my
life away
Falling into this cloud of grey
Watching me be more destructive day by day
Becoming another council estate cliché
And now I'm raising my voice
Cos I'm getting pissed off
Shouting a bit
Pounding on the wall a bit
Cos I'm pissed off
Telling her to get off my case
Get outta my face
Cos I'm pissed off

She says she just wants me to talk
Tell her how I'm feeling
Tell her what's going on
With me
I say I'd rather go for a walk

I can't help you if you don't tell me
Connor
Please

I'm like jeeeeeeeeeeez
What d'you want from me
I don't wanna talk
Why can't you just see
That I don't wanna talk

Just keeping on and on
You don't know where I'm coming from
Yet you keep
Going on and on
With the same old phenomenon

She goes, 'I can't force your dad to come
and see you
I wish that was something I could pursue'
A duck appears in the memory, more grown than before.
Connor looks at it. It disappears.

I cut her off

Glitch.

I cut her off
Make her stop
I'm not gunna stand here and take a lecture
from some pure hypocrite
Because yeah, I may be dealing with some
shit

But who are you
To be telling me what to do

Well I'm your mother you fool

I say yeah that's cool
But guess what?
I don't need you

Beat.

She leaves the clothes for a sec
Walks towards me
Eyes all glossy
Slams the kitchen door
And now it's war
I see red

Who is she to push and push
Poke and prod
But don't like it when I tell her the truth
That she ain't my God
She ain't my dad

But now I'm mad
Cos in my face she's just closed the door
So I open it
And without a minute to think
A loud BANG is heard. Flashing lights. Black.

I stamp her to the floor

Running

Trizzy's Freestyle kicks in.

Musician is drumming like a heartbeat getting more intense and it fills the space as the spotlight on Connor comes up.

He's stood there frozen still. The horror at what he's just done.

The void starts to close in on him as he runs, becoming more claustrophobic like the past is catching up with him.

CONNOR   Time
             just
                slows
                       down
           To where it freezes completely
           Momentarily
           I just stand there
                       Frozen
           Unable to move
               Utter disbelief
           I just stare.
           Mum on the floor
                       next to the chair.
           Seconds ticking away
               Tick Tock
                       Tick Tock
           Feeling like a life sentence.
           Shackling me
                       Suffocating me
               Devouring me

Shock

Horror

Fear
At what I just done
Who I've just become.

A million thoughts

racing through my head
Image of Mum on the floor
Is piercing me at my core

My whole mind goes
silent

Only thought
Why the fuck did I turn violent?
So

in that moment,
Looking at what I just done
Only thing I can think to do is
run

So
I sprint
Without a second to think
Out the door
Leaving her on the floor

Run down the street

Running
> *Running*

take a right
> Whole body getting tight

I'm anxious
> fright

I run
Running
> Running

Everything becomes a blur
Thinking how the fuck could I do that to her
> Disbelief
>> coursing through my veins

Through my thoughts
How the hell could you just leave her
> there on the floor

All alone
> In pain

Why the fuck didn't you check if she was ok?

Haunting image.
> Won't leave my thoughts

It's etched in brick.
Following me
> as
>> I'm running.

Thinking you absolute *prick*

So I carry on
    running
       running.
Running
    and
    running.

Through the rain
    real wet and thick
To escape these thoughts.

I run
    Down Corpa Road
I'm in
    full Usain Bolt mode
Pegging it
    towards George Street Bridge
Starting to get a stitch
       No guidance
No idea
    of where I'm going
      What I'm doing.

I'm running
    through alleyways
   over walls and across roads.
Narrowly swerving
in
    and

out
of cars
Who the fuck knows.

Heart beat's racing.
cars are chasing
horns are beeping.
As I'm leaping
Over the bonnets of the cars
Strangers are swearing
cursing at me

Underneath the stars
I dart
across the stampede
through Kemp Park
running
running
running
running
running
legs starting to feel numb
All I'm thinking
is what I've just done to my mum

cut through some bushes
down a lane
Onto a street that is sorta familiar
A street that can

hopefully
take
away this pain

Drawn to this door
like some sort of juju
Enticing me in
open the gate

Approach the door
Deja vu
Have I been here before?
Ball up my fist
And

Knock

Open the door

Connor knocks frantically on the front door. Urgency behind this.

There's a life or death feel. Connor can be saved (so he thinks) if the door is opened.

CONNOR   Yo, Quick, Hello, Open up
Dad!?

Fuck
I got
feds
on me
it's not funny
I just

need
        somewhere.
I fucked up I done some dumb shit, I can't
ask Mum, I just need some *help*.

Remember that time you promised
we'd go to feed the ducks
you didn't
I forgave you
... please.
Fucked up.
Need a dad.
you hate me calling you
   (but)
      It's fact.

Dad, I fucked up
blinked
Yeah.
   Didn't think
Yeah.

Won't take any of your time
mix you a Sunset; your overproof and lime
when it's time for tea – I pray you
make me your chicken rice and peas.

I won't take space
You won't even notice

I'll respect the rules
     of your house.

I'm scared
    Full on scared
Don't know what to do
Kept running
    and running
       For miles

Legs,
    brought me here
       is this your house?
Or
    you just renting it out?
Please
open the door
    I'll sleep on your floor
        Won't be no
     bother
No
    trouble
        No cuddles
Please
   please
     open the door

A creep of light like a curtain being drawn above. Father peeking through the window.

Why you treating me like some animal at
the zoo?
fuck this
        fuck you
                I'm outta here
Don't need this
Definitely
don't need you
Keep your fucking flat
        cos it's trash
    You're lucky
right now
                I'd swing and I'd mash

Don't be sat
on your almighty high horse
Thinking you're
            God
Cos I know some things
    yeah
                I ain't dumb
Know exactly
        what you did
to
Mum

        Tears in her eyes
bullshit
                lies

You put her through
Got her
   Others
           Different women
all handling your *dick*
   Not
   knowing
you
   full on prick
Going from
woman
   to woman
      to woman
   full of cum
waste man,

Yeah

       Bum

Fuck this
   I'm out
      done
Don't deserve for me to be your son.

Connor sits on the curb outside his father's house. Rejected.

In a trance breathing deep.

A duck darts across the street. Looks at Connor.

CONNOR   The fuck do you want?

Connor's lost in thought.

Rave occurs in the street outside his father's house. Dancing in a trance of rejection.

Without a Dad init

Intro

You see

Life can be real fucking hard without a dad in it.

Proper messed up.

Like you go through trials and tribulations and shit.

Without a dad in it.

You lash out.

And you fight and you hit

Because without a positive male role model well,

life's just shit.

Chorus Intro

Life is just fucking shit

Without a dad in it, without a dad init? Question everything

Without a dad in it, without a dad init?

Every day struggling

Without a dad in it, without a dad init? Every day muggling

Without a dad in it, without a dad init?

Verse 1

So the questions
you ask yourself.

piece it together
the answers.
You search for
To make you better

But you torture yourself
Torture yourself
Seeking answers
To cure the cancer
That's inside

The questions. The questions
Running through your mind
The insecurities.
They're far from kind.
But they're constantly there.
Constantly there

Like a disease. Just chipping away.
At your core
Bit by bit.

Because all you want is that little bit more
So you ask yourself

Chorus

Why's life fucking shit
Without a dad in it, without a dad init?
Question everything
Without a dad in it, without a dad init?

Every day struggling
Without a dad in it, without a dad init?
Every day muggling
Without a dad in it, without a dad init?

Verse 2

The questions they go like this
Why me? Why me?
What did I do? What did I do?
Why aren't I good enough?
Why aren't I good enough enough

Why don't you love me?
Why don't you love me?
Where did you go? Where did you go?
And
Why did you go? Why did you go?
And it's always that
Why
That Why
That Why
That Why
That Why
That Why
Why
Why
Why
Why
Why
Why

Why!?

Chorus

Because life is just full on shit

Without a dad in it, without a dad init?
Question everything

Without a dad in it, without a dad init?
Every day struggling

Without a dad in it, without a dad init?
Every day muggling

Without a dad in it, without a dad init?
My life was just full on shit

Without my dad init.

*Connor is in a full on trance with no care in the world.
Dancing free like it could be his last dance.*

Red and blue flashing lights surround him.

*Connor kneels on the ground with his hands behind his
head accepting his fate.*

POLICE OFFICER Connor Allen

I'm arresting you on suspicion of assault
and battery and GBH

You do not have to say anything but it may
harm your defence if you do not mention
when questioned something which you
later rely on in court.

Anything you do say may be given in
evidence

You are being charged with two counts
of assault and battery and one count of
Grievous Bodily Harm.

How do you plead?

Projections of the following information fill the void as the sounds of the door throb and throb in the background:

Assault and Battery – the action of threatening a person together with the action of making physical contact with them.

Grievous Bodily Harm a crime in which one person does serious physical injury to another.

Voicemail to Nan

Sounds of a phone ringing. The sound of the voice fills the void.

Everything else is black.

ANSWERING MACHINE You   have   reached   the
answering machine

We are unable to come to the phone right now

but please leave your message after the beep and we'll get back to you at the earliest convenience

Beep.

CONNOR   Hey,

Nan,

I was just wondering if

Well I was hoping

I need your help

Cos I... I

I don't know if you've spoken to Mum

Yet

But I'm down Maindee Police Station

I've messed up and like

Please

I had no one else to turn to

There's only you

I'm sorry ok

For everything

I... just... yeah

If you can come that would be great

Like

Come and get me

Please

I love you Nan

End of message.

No Comment

Lights up on Connor in the interview room at the police station. The police officer is sat by a table with a recording machine on it. The musician or void can become the solicitor from high above.

POLICE OFFICER Ah Mr Allen, sit down

Interview starting at 20:07

I am recording this interview for evidence should this case go to trial

The date is the 2nd July 2007

Location is Maindee Police Station

This is an interview with ...

Beat.

>Can you state your full name please?

CONNOR No comment

SOLICITOR Connor Allen

POLICE OFFICER For the record let that be known that that was the voice of Connor's solicitor as he is a minor.

>Can you state your date of birth please?

CONNOR No comment

SOLICITOR Fourteenth of the sixth Nineteen ninety-two

POLICE OFFICER At the conclusion of the interview, I will give you a form which will explain the procedure for dealing with this recording and how you can have access to it.

>Now, where were you this evening between the times of 15:00pm and 18:00pm Connor?

CONNOR No comment

POLICE OFFICER For the purpose of the recording I am showing Connor a picture of Person A

>Do you know this woman?

CONNOR No comment

POLICE OFFICER For the purpose of the recording I am showing Connor exhibits A, B and C which are photographic evidence of the injuries the victim, person A sustained

>Do you know how this woman got these cuts and bruises sustained in these photographs?

CONNOR No comment

POLICE OFFICER Look, Connor,

> We can't help you if you don't tell us what went on. We need to know your side of events
>
> And you saying 'No comment' isn't helping us piece together these events

CONNOR   No comment

POLICE OFFICER Records show that this woman in the picture is your mother

CONNOR   No comment

POLICE OFFICER So you had a fight with your mother?

CONNOR   No comment

POLICE OFFICER So it's just you and Mum at home

> Oh,
>
> And a younger brother if I'm correct

CONNOR   No comment

POLICE OFFICER Just the three of you

> No dad in the picture?

CONNOR   No

> Comment

POLICE OFFICER Right,

> Whose flat were you banging on when we found you?

CONNOR   No comment

POLICE OFFICER Anyone you know?

CONNOR   No comment

POLICE OFFICER Well as you've used your phone call and no one has come to bail you out you'll have to stay in the cell overnight

> Interview terminated at 20:12

Connor exits. Sound of cell door slamming shut.

Ducking the police

Connor falls through the cell door and is falling and falling, like he is suspended in time. Trying to claw his way back up to escape.

He has fallen into his thoughts and is falling deeper and deeper.

Ducks are climbing from the bottom, rising and rising, trying to drag him down and keep him there.

Connor is fighting to get back to reality but the ducks are submerging him. Suffocating him.

He is alone with his thoughts and insecurities.

The voids start to rip open and bleed into each other. Lights flash.

Connor's going mad. Nightmare. Blackness.

Different Connors from all points of his timestream are bleeding through, shouting the words below.

Quacking.

It should feel like they are all vying for attention. Shouting over each other. The voices fill the universe. He is going insane with all the thoughts.

CONNOR   Why me?

What did I do?

Why am I not good enough?

Why am I different?

What is wrong with me?

Why am I feeling this way?

Why am I not loved?

Why am I not wanted?

Why doesn't he want me?

Why am I like this?

What have I got to do?

Who's going to pick me up when I'm low?
How do I grow?

Why am I different?

Why aren't I accepted?

Why do I feel like this?

I don't want to be different

How do I become a man?

Who's going to show me who I'm meant to be?

How do I understand that I'm different?

How do I understand why I'm different?
How do I make this go away?

Where do I fit in?

Am I a monster?

Voicemail from Nan

Returning to the void.

Connor bursts out of a door and is breathing frantically. He has escaped the nightmare but is broken.

CONNOR   Yo, can we get the lights up? Can't see *(to stage manager)*

He looks around and frantically tries to calm himself and figure out where he is. Searching through the scattered parts of his life. This can take as long as needed.

A message from Nan plays out.

NAN	Yeah I remember your voicemail.
	That night.
	Like it was yesterday.
	Don't forget something like that darling.
	Me and your grandfather sat around the kitchen table and we discussed what to do
	With you.
	I wanted to come and get you but your grandfather insisted. He said, 'No love I'm going to get him because for once in his life he needs a man'.
	I'll never forget that
	Just when I thought I couldn't love him anymore
CONNOR	Yeah. Me too. I never knew he said that
NAN	Yeah. And then he went and picked you up and brought you here.
	I gave you the biggest hug when I saw you because I knew you just needed love. Needed to know you were loved.
	You just needed to know that it was going to be ok.
CONNOR	Love you Nan
NAN	Love you too
	So this is going to be in your story?

Connor looks at the audience.

CONNOR   Yeah Nan

Connor stops for a moment.

All the doors are now titled 5th July 2007. The void is becoming more unstable. Connor goes through a door.

The fight - Jonny

Connor goes through the door and back to the memory.
Lliswerry High School, 5th July 2007.

CONNOR   There's something really weird going back
to the jungle

Especially after spending days up with my nan

Because I wasn't a fan

Of returning home.

Through the ugly green gates

Back into the rumble

that is school

No more trying to act cool

Not when you're the black sheep

Open secret lingering in the air

Everyone acting like they care

Really it ain't fair

Because

it's all fake

they don't actually care it's all just an act
They've heard about

me giving Mum a smack

Want the gossip and the facts

I walk down the halls

Swagger's gone for the time being

I roll my eyeballs

Stroll into the form room

Energy is different

Same animals in the same flutters

Hanging in their same clutters
But amongst all that you hear the mutters

Clear as day
When the bell goes at three
Jonny's coming for you
To fuck you up in the field across the road
He's gonna be in full-on beast mode

The field across the road
all the fights take place
Scores get settled
In an arena of stingy nettles
The whole animal kingdom gather to see
who reigns supreme for a brief moment
in time

So I go about my day
The energy still weird
following me from lesson to lesson
It's a blessing
when one or two animals from the hood
ask me if I'm good
saying they're rooting for me
And would help me if they could
Day passes
Jonny won't risk doing anything inside
of school
Won't risk an exclusion
Or any confusion

That he's the top lion
Wants an audience on a grand scale
so he can fuck me up without fail
Knock me out... looking pale
But I know I can do him damage
Not being cocky

He gets twisted up on the estate
For trying to act great
Always chatting bare shit
But three o clock rings
A stampede marches over to the field across
the road
I'm like mate the last thing we gotta do is hit
He's like

JONNY   there's a code
CONNOR   Looking at him and he's shaking with anger
In full-on beast mode
I've seen that before in his eyes
When I looked in the mirror

Before I know it we're scrapping
Don't even know what's happening
But I drop him
With a right hook
He didn't have time to look
A circle of bodies are forming around us
making an arena
yelling encouragement like a pack of hyenas

He gets up and is grappling me like John Cena
Fists are flying
I'm desperately trying
To kick Jonny's head in
He's trying to kick mine in too

He doesn't have a clue
The shit I been through

Minds drifting
Odds are shifting

One pound
Two pound
Three pound
Four on the jaw
I'm on the floor
Looking up at the sky
Thinking to myself why?

Why did I do that to my mum?
Lay there thinking
Just take the beating
What I deserve

Spit my blood on the graffitied concrete wall
I'm laying there on the floor
Sounds of the animals filling the void.
This beating is something I can't avoid

> Enough is enough
>
> A few of Jonny's cronies grab him off me
> He's won the fight,
>
> that's clear
>
> everyone can see.
>
> The arena disperses
>
> I make my way home for tea
>
> See
>
> we ain't been living together
>
> I been up Aunty's and Nan's
>
> Haven't spoken since it happened
>
> Today's the day she's expecting me
>
> Mum is
>
> To come home for tea

Connor goes through the front door of the house and enters the courtroom. Memories are starting to merge. The void is breaking down.

All Rise

Newport Magistrates Courtroom, 2nd August 2007.

CONNOR   All rise

sentencing day is here

All rise

And buried below is the fear

All rise

At what's going to become of me

All rise

All I can do is wait and see

All rise

With pictures as evidence all around me
All rise
constantly reminding me
All rise
Getting so nervous that I have to pee
All rise
Mum's sitting across from me
With a solicitor sitting next to her
And my solicitor leans over to confer
Then approaches the judge's bench
to hand over a Letter with grades attached
Off a handful of teachers but there's a catch
Don't let Connor become part of the juvenile system they plead
We don't want to mislead, just look and read up on his potential

Mum agrees
Mum sees
The teachers' plea
The belief in me
Even after everything I've done
The monster I become
She's sat across from me still fighting for me
Still believing in me
Like my own army seeing the good in me
I look at her
Amongst all the atmosphere tear rolling down her cheek

And a smile on her face as she looks back at me

The judge says, 'All rise'

Looks at me and says that he is strongly advising

That the days of me brutalising

Are from this day forth behind me

Because he can see

That many people have faith in me

None more than my mum

Who's been beneficial in his decision and outcome

So with that being said

Connor Allen you're found guilty of the charges I just read

But instead

Of failing you and putting you in jail

With other hotheads

I am giving you a 3-year suspended sentence

And what I mean by that

Is that you can't get in any trouble for that length of time

Not even a warning

Or basically your ass will be mine

And if you can do that

Then your record will be wiped

So it's now down to you

To grow from everything you've been through

It's essential to show all the people who believe in you

And your credentials and your potential

That they're right to believe in the good in you

Case closed.

The Judge bangs a wooden hammer for the verdict and the case is settled. The courtroom disperses.

Then three more bangs ring out. Distinct. Singular. With each bang the padlocked door draws nearer and nearer from the back of the void. A voice is bleeding through the door.

VOICE   That's real good cake.

CONNOR   No No No

Make it stop

Please make it stop

Anyone, make it stop.

Running out of time

Can't run no more

Gotta face the repercussions

Of what I done

No... *No!*

Connor tries to rewind back through his timestream. Restart again. But it doesn't work.

It's here. The void is breaking down.

No more running. No more rewinding.

Connor turns to face the padlocked door. He can't run anymore.

Connor acknowledges the grey duck that's been following him for the first time.

This is it

The door to 6th July 2007 is opened revealing a cafe, and Connor's father is waiting there for him eating red velvet cake.

FATHER   That's good cake

CONNOR   This mine?

FATHER   Well you wanted carrot cake

Connor enters the cafe and goes back to the memory.

CONNOR   Thanks

Silence to the point it becomes uncomfortable.

FATHER   So...

CONNOR   So...

FATHER   You going to say anything?

CONNOR   Like?

FATHER   Your mum said you had questions

CONNOR   Not really

FATHER   Right

CONNOR   What?

FATHER   Well we both know that isn't true

CONNOR   ...

FATHER   Why'd you do it?

CONNOR   What?

FATHER   You know what. Why?

CONNOR   Thanks for the birthday card

FATHER   I asked you a question.

CONNOR   I just wanna come, live with you?

FATHER   Is that a joke?

CONNOR   No

FATHER   Are you mad?

CONNOR   No

I'm being serious
I hate it at home.

Beat.

CONNOR   Mum doesn't understand
FATHER   That really is good cake that.
My favourite
CONNOR   She just doesn't get it
She doesn't understand me.
FATHER *(laughs)* What? and you think I will?
Think I have all the answers
CONNOR   Guess so.
Yeah.
FATHER   Think you're a big man these days d'you?
CONNOR   No
FATHER   Clearly
Smacking women now.
Your mum of all people.
CONNOR   It wasn't like that
FATHER   If you can do that to your mum
The woman who is there for you
Does everything for you
What are you capable of doing to me?
That's what goes through my head.
That's why you ain't coming to live with me
CONNOR   But I'd never do that to you
FATHER   I've already had a stroke I don't need that at my age/
CONNOR   /I wouldn't do anything like that though
Not to you.

FATHER   Look at you. You're a monster. I don't/

CONNOR   /A MONSTER?!

FATHER   Lower your voice

CONNOR   Or what?

FATHER   Or nothing.

                 Lower your voice.

                 I ain't your mother for starters.

                 I ain't putting up with your shit.

Beat.

                 And quite frankly me scared of you.

CONNOR   Maybe you should look in the mirror

Beat.

FATHER   Scared of what you'll do

CONNOR   But I ain't gunna do anything

                 How hard is that to understand

                 I just wanna come and live with you

FATHER   Right

                 And what am I meant to say to my wife?

CONNOR   What?

FATHER   Yeah.

                 My wife.

                 I'll just say oh here's my son that you don't know exists and he's going to come and live with us

                 ...

                 Don't look at me like that.

                 You wanted the truth so you're getting the truth

                 You're old enough.

Life's complex ok

Sooner you accept that the better

You can't come and live with me and that's that

I'm not going to be this loving dad that will push you on a swing and talk to you about life and being a man and teach you to shave and all that crap

Give you all the answers to the questions you have

Just ain't gunna happen

One day you'll understand

CONNOR Understand what?

Beat.

FATHER That the only person you can rely on is yourself.

My father wasn't around and I'm doing fine.

Plenty of kids grow up without their dads and they're fine.

They don't go around beating up their mothers.

CONNOR Right.

Well... FYI red velvet cake is shit.

Connor gets up to leave.

FATHER *Sit* down

CONNOR I'm good

Enjoy your cake

Connor leaves the cafe and re-enters the void.

Connor looks back at his father.

(Both at the same time)

CONNOR   Am I a monster?

FATHER   You're a monster!

Monster in the mirror

The void is different. No more glitches and breakdowns.
A melody starts to kick in.

The cafe starts to retreat and Connor watches it disappear
He's freestyling his own destiny, a goodbye to the pain.

After years of running and rewinding he is finally free
and moving on.

CONNOR   I used to wish I could start again
And write a different story with my pen
But then I wouldn't be me
Free
To work out my identity

But who's the man you see
When you look in the mirror?
Who's the man you wanna be?
When you look past the bitter?
Because I finally know the man I want to be
If you're heads I wanna be tails
If you're yin I wanna be yang
If you're Thanos then I wanna be Iron Man
Completely opposite.
Nothing alike.
Nothing like you.
I want to be better.

As all I ever wanted was for you to just show me where I was meant to go.

Who I was meant to be.

Beat.

You really were a god to me

Beat.

I never wanted money in a birthday card or presents under the Christmas tree

I just wanted your time.

Your love.

Maybe even the occasional hug

On the rare occasions you were around I was petrified of closing my eyes

in case you left.

Silly I know

Beat.

But

Time is all I wanted.

Time to push me on a swing at Beechwood Park

Or kick a ball with me in the back yard

Time to see me play the shepherd in my reception Christmas show

read me a bedtime story.

The ugly duckling

Tell me a bad joke

Have me chuckling

I just wanted you to lie.

Say you love me so I'd know what that felt like.

To be loved

Beat.

You see.

I went to university.

Got an amazing job.

And I ain't gotta thank you for that.

It's down to the woman you abandoned with two kids.

It's down to Mum.

Because she was Mum and she was Dad. She was all I had

She never gave up on me.

And that makes her ten if not twenty times the man you'll ever claim to be.

Because all you saw was a broken kid that you never wanted to fix.

But
guess what I am fixed.

I am bruised.

I am brave.

I am strong.

And yes I am loved.

None of that is down to you.

Beat.

I spent so long idolising you, hating you.

It consumed me.
All that rage.

I don't need you.
Never have.
You were just a drake
Never there
It wasn't fair
I'll *never* be *you.*
I may look like you
That's outta my control but
I won't become you.

My babies will never have to wait by the door
Praying that the next knock is me
Because I will be there in their home cuddling them to sleep
Reading them a bedtime story
They won't be afraid to close their eyes and blink
When they open their eyes I will still be there

It's taken me so many years but I finally know what it's like to be *loved.*
Truly *loved.*
It takes a village to raise a child they say
And that's ok
Because I've had a great village
In Mum, Jodi, Aunty Helen, Nan

And so many more they all showed me how to be a man.

Connor is free. Transformed. A weight has been lifted and a cycle ended. Looking around at all his memories, he has tears of happiness.

The grey duck is transformed into a swan.

Connor picks up his graduation hat from university.

CONNOR   Did you know...

In the UK there are more black and mixed-race boys in prison than university

I was so close to becoming that statistic. But I got a second chance.

I went to university. I graduated.

And shoutout to my mum who raised two mixed-race kids on a Newport council estate and they both went to university

So shoutout to my brother too!

My mum, she carried me for nine.

My father well, never really had mine

But so many people gave me the gift of time And I understand finally/

Voices of past Connor. Echoes of the past.

ECHO OF PAST   /Am I a monster?

CONNOR   Am I a monster?

Connor is hearing his past. But no longer a prisoner of it. Standing in his present, Connor is free and this is the fullest and most honest version we see. He has done it. He has set himself free. He takes the question of his past and starts to play with it.

CONNOR　　Am I a monster for getting shit wrong?

Am I a monster for balling up my feelings and putting them in a poem or a song?

Am I a monster for taking thirty years to figure out where I belong?

Am I a monster?

One door creaks open and the voice of his mum echoes through like it's calling out and pulling Connor in.

MUM　　I still love you you're my son

CONNOR　　Mum?

Am I a monster?

Chorus

Am I a monster?

For getting things wrong

I ball up my feelings

and put them in a song

Thirty years later

I know where I belong

Am I a monster?

For getting things wrong

I ball up my feelings

and put them in a song

Thirty years later

I know where I belong

I'm sorry Mum

Verse 1

The shackles are off and now I'm living free

I'm the realest coldest version of me
Countless hours spent in therapy
I breathe in now count one two and three

Like Usher Raymond I must confess
Looking back at my past I was blessed
My heart my heart was put to the test
But after everything, Mum didn't love me
any less

Chorus

Am I a monster?
For getting things wrong
I ball up my feelings
and put them in a song
Thirty years later
I know where I belong

Am I a monster?
For getting things wrong
I ball up my feelings
and put them in a song
Thirty years later
I know where I belong
I'm sorry Mum

Verse 2

I'm mixed-race got the best of both worlds
Now I'm older I embrace all my curls
Transformation
Duck to a Swan

Newport Jamaica that's where man's come from

We're all human we all make mistakes
No longer waiting going to the duck lake
I'm talented confident as fuck
Wish I had this knowledge when I was growing up

Chorus

Am I a monster?
For getting things wrong
I ball up my feelings
and put them in a song
Thirty years later
I know where I belong

Am I a monster?
For getting things wrong
I ball up my feelings
and put them in a song
Thirty years later
I know where I belong
I'm sorry Mum

Am I a monster?
For getting things wrong
I ball up my feelings
and put them in a song
Thirty years later

I know where I belong

Thank you Mum.

Connor kisses the microphone and leaves it as he has spoken his final words. Lights fade down as Connor exits and smoke submerges the void until it's blackness.

A recording of Mum's voice pulls him in as he walks through the door to forgiveness and has finally broken the loop he has been on for fifteen years.

MUM   Well if I didn't forgive you, you wouldn't be around would you?

Going down that road, have you back in my life, I could say no

D'you know what I mean?

I look at it and think, yeah people make mistakes

Everybody makes mistakes in life

Everybody does

Nobody's perfect

If they say they are, that's a load of bullshit because nobody's perfect

If you didn't make mistakes you wouldn't grow up

You have to make mistakes to grow.

One final quack plays out.

Lights down.

The end.